The United States ABCs

WRITTEN BY:
Isla Bowens

ILLUSTRATED BY:
Elena Kochetova

STORK
PUBLISHING
HOUSE

IS FOR AMERICAN FLAG

Our nation's flag that proudly flies high in the wind.

is for Bald Eagle

Our nation's bird that symbolizes strength and freedom.

IS FOR CONSTITUTION

The supreme law of the land, that establishes the structure of the federal government and protects the people living here.

is for Declaration of Independence

THE FOUNDING DOCUMENT OF THE UNITED STATES OF AMERICA.

is for Equality

A concept that promotes an equal chance
of success for every individual.

is for Founding Fathers

B. FRANKLIN

G. WASHINGTON

T. JEFFERSON

J. MADISON

J. ADAMS

A. HAMILTON

THE MEN WHO CONTRIBUTED TO THE FOUNDING OF THE UNITED STATES.

is for Great Seal

Our nation's seal that symbolizes independence, strength, and unity.

is for Hard-Working

A TERM USED TO DESCRIBE THE HARD WORK PEOPLE PUT INTO THEIR
LIVES, JOBS, AND COMMUNITIES ALL ACROSS THIS COUNTRY.

IS FOR INDEPENDENCE DAY

A DAY ALSO KNOWN AS THE FOURTH OF JULY, WHERE OUR COUNTRY CELEBRATES ITS INDEPENDENCE FROM GREAT BRITAIN IN 1776.

IS FOR JUSTICE

An important value in our society that gives
everyone equal justice under the law.

IS FOR KNOWLEDGE

The ability to have the ease of access to a wide range of information about historical facts and events, our country's foundational documents, cultural heritage, and core values and beliefs.

is for Liberty Bell

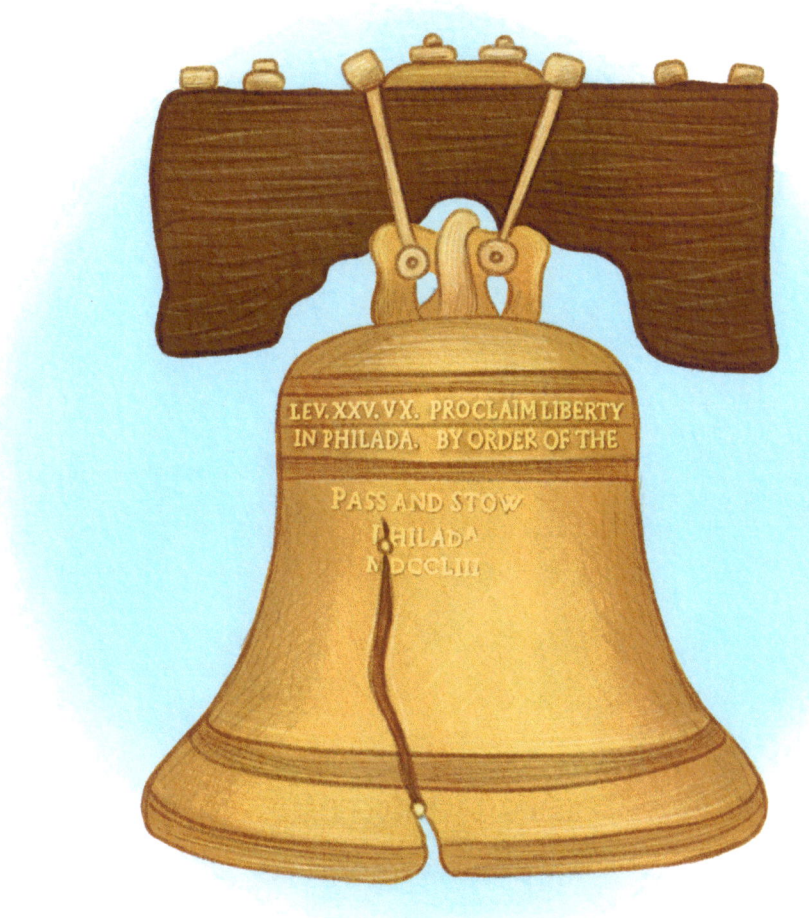

WHICH STANDS AS A SYMBOL OF LIBERTY AND FREEDOM
IN THE UNITED STATES, AND IS LOCATED IN PHILADELPHIA.

is for Multicultural

A TERM USED TO DESCRIBE THE DIVERSE PEOPLE FROM VARIOUS CULTURES WHO RESIDE IN THIS COUNTRY.

IS FOR NATIONALISM

The pride we have for our great country.

is for Oceans

The Atlantic, Pacific, and Arctic oceans
that surround the United States.

is for Patriotism

THE LOVE THAT WE HAVE FOR OUR GREAT COUNTRY, THE LOVE THAT WE HAVE FOR THE UNITED STATES OF AMERICA.

is for QUALITY of LIFE

A concept in which we, as the American people, choose to apply ourselves to achieve a high quality standard of living.

IS FOR RELIGION

WHICH EVERYONE IN THIS COUNTRY IS FREE
to PRACTICE AND IDENTIFY WITH.

is for Statue of Liberty

WHICH REPRESENTS OUR INDEPENDENCE, FREEDOM,
AND OPPORTUNITY, AND IS LOCATED IN NEW YORK CITY.

IS FOR THANKSGIVING

A HOLIDAY WE CELEBRATE THAT EXPRESSES
GRATITUDE FOR ALL OF LIFE'S BLESSINGS.

is for United States of America

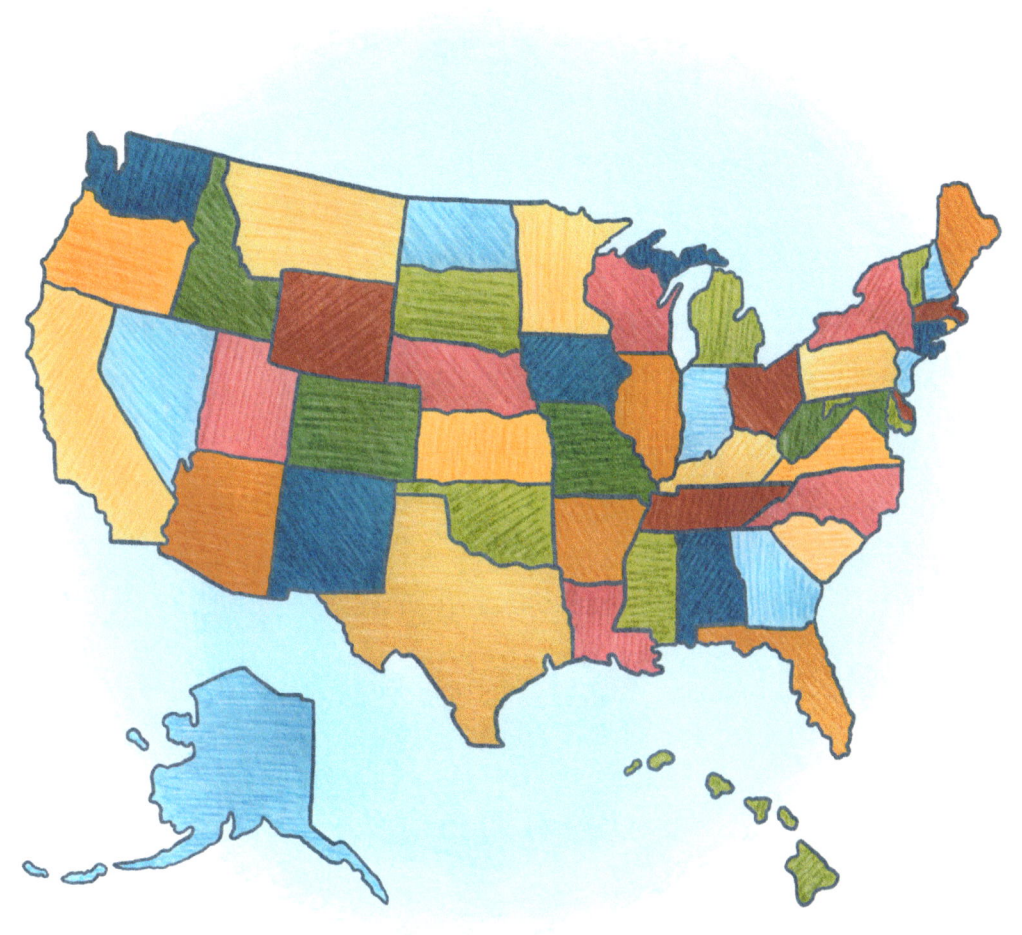

THE NAME OF OUR GREAT COUNTRY,
WHICH IS MADE UP OF 50 INDIVIDUAL STATES.

IS FOR VETERANS

The men and women of our country who served in the U.S. military.

is for Washington, D.C.

Our nation's capital city.

IS FOR XENIAL

The attitude of the citizens of this country that makes everyone—both native and foreign—feel comfortable and appreciated.

IS FOR YEAR-ROUND

THE ABILITY TO EXPERIENCE A DIFFERENT
SEASON—SPRING, SUMMER, FALL, AND WINTER

IS FOR ZONES

EASTERN, CENTRAL, MOUNTAIN, PACIFIC, ALASKA, AND HAWAII-ALEUTIAN ZONES ARE USED ACROSS THIS COUNTRY TO TELL TIME.

www.ingramcontent.com/pod-product-compliance
Lightning Source LLC
Chambersburg PA
CBHW041554120626
46551CB00002B/199